Developing Numeracy
USING AND APPLYING MATHS

INVESTIGATIONS FOR THE DAILY MATHS LESSON

year
5

Hilary Koll and Steve Mills

A & C BLACK

Mathematical skills and processes

Page	Activity title	Predict	Visualise	Look for pattern	Record	Reason	Make decisions	Estimate	Explain	Be systematic	Co-operate	Compare	Test ideas	Trial and improvement	Ask own questions	Generalise	Check	Simplify
Numbers and the number system																		
14	Fantastic fractions			●	○	○				●		○	○			○	○	
15	Chinese numbers	●	○	○		●			●		○	○				○		
16	Cracking percentages				○	●	●				○				○		○	
17	Trainspotting			●	○	○										●		
18	Making chains			●	○	○			○				○					
19	The fun factor			●	○	○				●		○				○		
20	What's going on?			○		●			○				●					
Calculations																		
21	Yo-ho-ho!				○	●			●		●	○						●
22	Billy's Fizz Factory		●		●				○	●		○					○	
23	Multiple choice	●		○		●			○			○	○			○		
24	Calculating creatures			○		●	○		○	○				●	○			
25	Daffodil dilemma	●			●	●		○				○						
26	Square subtractions			●		○	●					○	○	○				
27	Secret numbers	○			○	○	○	○				○		●			○	
28	A dog's life			○		●						●			○	○		
29	Digit patterns	○		●		○			○							●		
Solving problems																		
30	Shut that door!	○		●					●			○				○	○	
31	Let's go nuts!		○	○		●			○		○					○		●
32–33	Bell-ringers: 1 and 2			●	○				●			○				○		
34	Roll, roll, roll your dice		●		○	●			○	○	○				○			
Handling data																		
35	Find the key				○	○	●		○		●		●					○
36	Finger angles	●	○		○			●				○					●	
Measures, shape and space																		
37	Palindromic times	●			○		●			●		○				○		
38	What's my card?		○		○				●		●	●						
39	One man went to mow…		○	●		●		○				○	○					
40	The Dark Ages						●		○			○	○				○	
41	A lengthy challenge	○	○		○	○		●				○	○				●	
42	Time to reflect		●	○						○		○				●		
43	Trying tiles	○	●	●	○		○				○		○					
44	Diagonal cuts	○		●	○	○						○			○	●	●	
45	Friday the 13th			○		○			○			○	●			●		
46	Overground map		●		●								○					○
47–48	Shape shifters: 1 and 2		●		●	○							○	●				

● Key processes identified on the activity sheet   ○ Additional processes involved in the activity

Contents

Measures, shape and space

Published 2005 by A & C Black Publishers Limited
37 Soho Square, London W1D 3QZ
www.acblack.com

ISBN-10: 0-7136-7140-8
ISBN-13: 978-0-7136-7140-7

Copyright text © Hilary Koll and Steve Mills, 2005
Copyright illustrations © Pat Murray, 2005
Copyright cover illustration © Charlotte Hard, 2005
Editors: Lynne Williamson and Marie Lister
Designer: Heather Billin

The authors and publishers would like to thank Jane McNeill and Catherine Yemm for their advice in producing this series of books.

A CIP catalogue record for this book is available from the British Library.

Printed and bound in Great Britain by Cromwell Press Ltd, Trowbridge, Wiltshire.

A & C Black uses paper produced with elemental chlorine-free pulp, harvested from managed sustainable forests.

Introduction

Developing Numeracy: Using and Applying Maths is a series of seven photocopiable activity books designed to be used during the daily maths lesson. The books focus on using and applying mathematics, as referred to in the National Numeracy Strategy *Framework for teaching mathematics*. The activities are intended to be used in the time allocated to pupil activities during the main part of the lesson. They are designed to develop and reinforce the skills and processes that are vital to help children use and apply their maths.

Using and applying mathematics

There are several different components which make up the **content** of maths and form the bulk of any maths curriculum:

- **mathematical facts**, for example, a triangle has three sides;
- **mathematical skills**, such as counting;
- **mathematical concepts**, like place value.

For maths teaching to be successful, it is vital that children can *use* this mathematical content beyond their classroom, either in real-life situations or as a basis for further understanding. However, in order to do so, they require extra abilities over and above the mathematical content they have learned. These extra abilities are often referred to as the **processes** of mathematical activity. It is these processes which make mathematical content usable.

As an example, consider this question:
How many triangles are there in this shape?

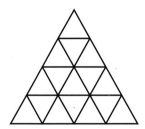

The mathematical content required is only:
- the **fact** that a triangle has three sides;
- the **skill** of counting.

As such, it could be expected that very young children could solve this problem. The fact that they cannot suggests that other abilities are involved. These are the processes, and for this question they include:
- visualising the different-sized triangles;
- being systematic in counting all the triangles of different sizes;
- looking for patterns in the numbers of triangles;
- trial and improvement;
- recording.

Unless children can apply these processes in this situation, then however good their counting skills and knowledge of triangles may be, they will fail.

The 'solving problems' strand of the *Framework for teaching mathematics* emphasises the importance of using and applying mathematics. This series of books is intended to make explicit the skills and processes involved in learning how to put maths knowledge to use.

Using and Applying Maths Year 5 supports the development of the using and applying processes by providing opportunities to introduce and practise them through a series of activities. On the whole these activities are designed for children to work on independently, although this is not always possible and occasionally some children may need support.

Pre-school children are naturally inquisitive about the world around them. They love to explore and experiment, and to make marks and record things on paper in their own idiosyncratic ways. Unfortunately, once at school the focus is often placed firmly on the maths content alone and children can be led to believe that maths is not a subject of exploration, but rather one of simply learning the 'right way to do things'. As a result, when older children are asked to explore and investigate maths they are often at a loss if their maths teaching to date has not encouraged and built upon their natural instincts.

Year 5 helps children to develop the following processes:
- predicting
- visualising
- looking for pattern
- recording
- reasoning
- making decisions
- estimating
- explaining
- being systematic
- co-operating
- comparing
- testing ideas
- trial and improvement
- asking own questions
- generalising
- checking
- simplifying

When using these activities, the focus need not be on the actual mathematical content. Instead, the teacher's demonstrations, discussions and questioning should emphasise the processes the children are using. A summary of the skills and processes covered by each activity is shown on page 2. When appropriate, invite the children to explain their thinking to others. Research has shown that children develop processes most successfully when the teacher encourages them to act as experts rather than novices, allowing them to work autonomously and encouraging a range of approaches to any problem rather than constraining discussion to produce an overall class plan. The children should evaluate their own plans against other plans in the posing, planning and monitoring phases of the lessons.

Extension

Many of the activity sheets end with a challenge (**Now try this!**) which reinforces and extends the children's learning, and provides the teacher with an opportunity for assessment. On occasion, it may be helpful to read the instructions with the children before they begin the activity. For some of the challenges the children will need to record their answers on a separate piece of paper.

Organisation

Very little equipment is needed, but it will be useful to have the following resources available: coloured pencils, counters, dice, scissors, coins, squared paper, hundred squares, number lines and number tracks.

To help teachers select appropriate learning experiences for the children, the activities are grouped into sections within the book. However, the activities are not expected to be used in this order unless stated otherwise. The sheets are intended to support, rather than direct, the teacher's planning.

Some activities can be made easier or more challenging by masking or substituting numbers. You may wish to re-use pages by copying them onto card and laminating them. If you find the answer boxes are too small for children's writing, you could enlarge the activity sheet onto A3 paper.

Teachers' notes

Brief notes are provided at the foot of each page giving ideas and suggestions for maximising the effectiveness of the activity sheets. These can be masked before copying.

Solutions and further explanations of the activities can be found on pages 7–13, together with examples of questions that you can ask.

Whole class warm-up activities

The following activities provide some practical ideas which can be used to introduce the main teaching part of the lesson.

Reasoning and being systematic

Choose a number between 1 and 100. Challenge the class to find out which number it is by asking questions such as *Is it a multiple of 5?* Praise questions that narrow down the field significantly, such as *Is it odd? Is it below 50?*, and questions that use mathematical language, such as *Is it divisible by three?* Encourage the children to work systematically towards the answer, and discourage wild guesses.

Generalising

Write some simple additions on the board: for example, $5 + 2 = 7$, $8 + 6 = 14$. Rewrite each statement underneath, substituting 'e' for 'even number' and 'o' for 'odd number':

$5 + 2 = 7$ $8 + 6 = 14$
$o + e = o$ $e + e = e$

Ask the children to write some more simple number statements in the same way. Discuss the patterns they notice.

Looking for pattern, testing ideas and explaining

On the board, draw a 4×5 grid with a measurement in each section, for example:

55 cm	0·72 m	8 cm	0·3 m	1 m
$\frac{1}{2}$ m	30 cm	0·35 m	72 cm	20 cm
7·2 m	0·5 m	0·2 m	50 cm	0·75 m
35 cm	92 cm	720 cm	$\frac{3}{4}$ m	45 cm

Ask the children to create number statements using the measurements in the grid: for example, $0·5 \, m = 50 \, cm$, $0·72 \, m = 72 \, cm$, $92 \, cm + 8 \, cm = 1 \, m$. (It can be useful to draw a blank grid on card and laminate it. New measurements can then be written in when required.)

Co-operating and making decisions

Write a number statement on the board, such as $30 \div 5 = 6$. Ask the children, working in pairs, to make up a story to match the statement: for example, *Thirty children are on a funfair ride. There are five children in each car and there are six cars.* Ask the class to decide which was the most interesting story.

Notes on the activities

Numbers and the number system

Fantastic fractions (page 14)

☆ *Processes: look for pattern, be systematic, record, reason, compare, test ideas, check*

Solutions:

2. (Rows can be in any order) ⟶

3. 4

4. (a) $\frac{2}{5}$

    (b) $\frac{5}{2}$

6. In the grid shown, the first row has the greatest total since all three fractions are improper fractions.

−	$\frac{3}{2}$	$\frac{4}{2}$	$\frac{5}{2}$
$\frac{2}{3}$	−	$\frac{4}{3}$	$\frac{5}{3}$
$\frac{2}{4}$	$\frac{3}{4}$	−	$\frac{5}{4}$
$\frac{2}{5}$	$\frac{3}{5}$	$\frac{4}{5}$	−

The same patterns occur for other sets of digits, i.e. the smallest fraction is the smallest digit over the largest digit, and the largest fraction is the largest digit over the smallest digit.

Suggested questions:
- What patterns do you notice?
- What if we tried different digits?

Chinese numbers (page 15)

☆ *Processes: predict, reason, explain, visualise, look for pattern, co-operate, compare, generalise*

The completed grid looks like this:

一	二	三	四	五	六	七	八	九	十
十一	十二	十三	十四	十五	十六	十七	十八	十九	二十
二十一	二十二	二十三	二十四	二十五	二十六	二十七	二十八	二十九	三十
三十一	三十二	三十三	三十四	三十五	三十六	三十七	三十八	三十九	四十
四十一	四十二	四十三	四十四	四十五	四十六	四十七	四十八	四十九	五十
五十一	五十二	五十三	五十四	五十五	五十六	五十七	五十八	五十九	六十
六十一	六十二	六十三	六十四	六十五	六十六	六十七	六十八	六十九	七十
七十一	七十二	七十三	七十四	七十五	七十六	七十七	七十八	七十九	八十
八十一	八十二	八十三	八十四	八十五	八十六	八十七	八十八	八十九	九十
九十一	九十二	九十三	九十四	九十五	九十六	九十七	九十八	九十九	一百

All the numbers from 1 to 99 are written using combinations of the symbols for 1 to 10. Eleven is 'ten one', twelve is 'ten two', and so on. Twenty is 'two ten', twenty-one is 'two ten one', and so on up to 99.

A Chinese number converter can be found on www.mandarintools.com/numbers.html

Suggested questions:
- How do you know that you have used the right symbols?
- What made you use that symbol?
- Can you explain how Chinese numbers work?

Cracking percentages (page 16)

☆ *Processes: reason, make decisions, co-operate, record, ask own questions, check*

To introduce this activity, first revise questions such as: 'What is 50% of 6… 25% of 8… 10% of 10… 20% of 5,' and so on. Then write the words 'SHOP' 'BREAD' and 'DOORSTEP' on the board. Give an example of how to crack this type of code by demonstrating how the first 50% of SHOP, the middle 20% of BREAD and the last 25% of DOORSTEP spell the word 'SHEEP'.

The coded messages on the activity sheet are 'WAIT FOR ME' and 'WHEREABOUTS?'

Suggested prompt:
- Try making up a message of your own in code.

Trainspotting (page 17)

☆ *Processes: look for pattern, generalise, reason, record*

This activity helps children to understand and develop tests of divisibility: for example, knowing that the sum of the digits of multiples of 3 are always multiples of 3.

Where sums are two-digit numbers also, the children could explore what happens if you find the sums of those digits.

Solutions:

Multiples of 2 – pattern 2, 4, 6, 8, 1, 3, 5, 7, 9 … even numbers then odd numbers then even, and so on.

Multiples of 3 – sums of digits are multiples of 3: for example, 3, 6, 9, 3, 6 …

Multiples of 4 – pattern 4, 8, 3, 7, 2, 6, 10, 5, 9 … alternate numbers go down in ones.

Multiples of 5 – pattern 5, 1, 6, 2, 7, 3, 8, 4, 9, 5 … alternate numbers go up in ones.

Multiples of 6 – sums of digits are multiples of 3: for example, 6, 3, 9, 6, 3, 9 …

Multiples of 7 – pattern 7, 5, 3, 10, 8, 6, 13, 11, 9 (if the digits of the two-digit numbers are added together, the pattern is 7, 5, 3, 1, 8, 6, 4, 2, 9 …)

Multiples of 8 – pattern 8, 7, 6, 5, 4, 12, 11, 10, 9 … numbers go down in ones.

Multiples of 9 – pattern 9, 9, 9, 9, 9, 9, 9, 9 … numbers are all multiples of 9.

Multiples of 10 – pattern 1, 2, 3, 4, 5, 6, 7, 8, 9 … numbers go up in ones.

Multiples of 11 – pattern 2, 4, 6, 8, 10, 12, 14, 16, 18 … numbers go up in twos.

Multiples of 12 – pattern 3, 6, 9, 12, 6, 9, 12, 15 … numbers are all multiples of 3 (if the digits of the two-digit numbers are added together, the pattern is 3, 6, 9, 3, 6, 9…)

Suggested questions:
- What patterns can you see?
- How could you explain that to someone else?
- How could you use this to help you recognise multiples of a number?

Making chains (page 18)

☆ *Processes: look for pattern, explain, reason, record, test ideas*

No number appears in more than one chain.

Solutions:

12→15→21→24→30→33→39→51→57→69→84→96→111
14→19→29→40→44→52→59→73→83→94→107
16→23→28→38→49→62→70→77→91→101
18→27→36→45→54→63→72→81→90→99→117
20→22→26→34→41→46→56→67→80→88→104
31→35→43→50→55→65→76→89→106

The numbers 53, 64, 75, 86 and 97 cannot be made from smaller starting numbers.

To understand why numbers appear in only one chain, it is sometimes useful to look at consecutive start numbers, for example:

12 + 3 = 15	43 + 7 = 50
13 + 4 = 17	44 + 8 = 52
14 + 5 = 19	45 + 9 = 54
15 + 6 = 21	46 + 10 = 56

It is clear that it will not be possible to make 54 from any number other than 45, since 44 makes a lower even number and 46 makes a higher even number.

Odd numbers are always produced from start numbers with an odd tens digit. Even numbers are always produced from start numbers with an even tens digit.

Suggested questions:
- What other patterns can you see?
- What happens to numbers whose digits add up to 10?
- What does that look like on a hundred square?

The fun factor (page 19)

☆ *Processes: look for pattern, be systematic, reason, record, compare, generalise*

Solutions:

1.

Number	Number of factors	Number	Number of factors	Number	Number of factors
1	1	11	2	21	4
2	2	12	6	22	4
3	2	13	2	23	2
4	3	14	4	24	8
5	2	15	4	25	3
6	4	16	5	26	4
7	2	17	2	27	4
8	4	18	6	28	6
9	3	19	2	29	2
10	4	20	6	30	8

2. 4, 9, 25
3. 2
4. 24

The numbers 1, 4, 9, 16 and 25 (and any square number) have an odd number of factors.

Suggested questions:
- What other patterns can you see?
- Can you explain why square numbers have an odd number of factors?

What's going on? (page 20)

☆ *Processes: reason, test ideas, look for pattern, explain*

This activity involves multiplying a number by 7, then 11, then 13, which is the same as multiplying by 1001. This has the effect of changing a three-digit number into a six-digit number with the original digits repeated: for example, 682 becomes 682 682. This is because 682 × 1000 = 682 000, and an additional 682 makes 682 682. The effect on two-digit numbers is as follows: 62 becomes 62 062.

As a further extension, the children could investigate multiplying by other numbers: for example, multiplying two-, three- or four-digit numbers by 73 and then by 137, or two-, three-, four- or five-digit numbers by 11 and then by 9091. Encourage them to explore the combined multiplication and to explain the final effect.

Suggested questions:
- What do you notice? Why do you think this happens?
- What happens to a number when we multiply it by 1000?
- What other numbers might have a similar effect when multiplied?

Calculations

Yo-ho-ho! (page 21)

☆ *Processes: reason, co-operate, explain, test ideas, record, simplify*

Talk to the class about rules for working in a group: each child should be given the opportunity to have their say; one person could be chosen to make notes; and everyone should make sure they can explain their answers to the rest of the class.

Gold coins		Gold earrings	
Peggy	Will	Jake	Dan
5	7	4	5

Maggoty biscuits		Treasure maps	
John	Tim	Jack	Mary
6	6	7	5

Suggested questions/prompts:
- Tell us about how your group worked together.
- What did your group do well?
- Did you have any difficulties?

Billy's Fizz Factory (page 22)

☆ *Processes: visualise, record, be systematic, explain, compare, check*

The chart shows possible ways of weighing amounts of fizz up to 20 kg (numbers indicate number of weights used):

f (kg)	10 kg	7 kg	f (kg)	10 kg	7 kg
1	2 + f	3	11	1 + f	3
2	4 + f	6	12	4	4 + f
3	1	1 + f	13	2	1 + f
4	1 + f	2	14	0 + f	2
5	3 + f	5	15	2 + f	5
6	2	2 + f	16	3	2 + f
7	0 + f	1	17	1	1
8	2 + f	4	18	1 + f	4
9	3	3 + f	19	4	3 + f
10	1	0 + f	20	2	0 + f

It is possible to weigh out any whole number amount in this way, because once it has been established that a 1 kg mass can be measured, then any other whole number amount in kilograms can be made, provided a limitless number of weights can be used.

Suggested questions/prompts:
- Is there more than one way to do this?
- Compare your solutions with your partner's.
- Do you think it is possible to weigh any whole number amount in kilograms using these weights? Why?

Multiple choice (page 23)
☆ *Processes: predict, reason, test ideas, look for pattern, explain, compare, generalise*

Children should notice that for all multiples that are factors of 100, they can divide 100 by the number to find how many multiples there will be: for example, 100 ÷ 5 = 20, so there will be 20 multiples of 5 between 1 and 100.

For multiples that are not factors of 100, division can still be used: for example, 100 ÷ 7 = 14 r 2, so there will be 14 multiples of 7. The remainder is ignored.

Solutions:			
multiples of 5	20	multiples of 10	10
multiples of 4	25	multiples of 2	50
multiples of 3	33	multiples of 8	12
multiples of 7	14	multiples of 6	16
multiples of 1	100	multiples of 9	11

There are 20 multiples of 15 between 1 and 300.

Suggested questions:
- What patterns did you notice in the numbers?
- Does it work for every multiple?
- What other predictions can you make?

Calculating creatures (page 24)
☆ *Processes: reason, trial and improvement, look for pattern, make decisions, explain, be systematic, ask own questions*

Solutions:

dog 364	bat 228	ram 726	bee 233	emu 368	pig 744
rat 728	yak 925	hen 436	sow 769	elk 355	fox 369
cow 269	hog 464	ewe 393	eel 335	gnu 468	kid 543

The children can explore this idea further by finding the total of more than two creatures. This might produce totals above 1999 and thus new words may be found (for example, 2253 = BAKE).

Suggested questions:
- Which words have you found?
- Why did you decide to stop working this one out? How did you know that it wouldn't work?
- Why did you rule out some of the words?
- What about totals greater than 1000?
- Which is the largest/smallest total that would make a real word?

Daffodil dilemma (page 25)
☆ *Processes: predict, record, reason, estimate, test ideas*
This activity allows children to see how numbers can grow very quickly when results are continually doubled.

Solution: 17 years
10→20→40→80→160→320→640→1280→2560→5120 →10 240→20 480→40 960→81 920→163 840→327 680→ 655 360→1 310 720

If 20 bulbs were planted, it would take 16 years.
If 40 bulbs were planted, it would take 15 years.
If 160 bulbs were planted, it would take 13 years.

When working out answers to the extension activity, the children should round decimals to the nearest whole number. Solutions:

10 bulbs – 20 years
10→18→32→58→104→187→337→607→1093→1967→ 3541→6374→11 473→20 651→37 172→66 910→120 438 →216 788→390 218→702 392→1 264 306

100 bulbs – 16 years
100→180→324→583→1049→1888→3398→6116→ 11 009→19 816→35 669→64 204→115 567→208 021→ 374 438→673 988→1 213 178

Suggested questions:
- How did you set out your work?
- Compare your working out with a partner's. Whose is easier to understand?

Square subtractions (page 26)
☆ *Processes: look for pattern, make decisions, reason, compare, test ideas, trial and improvement*

The children should be encouraged to look for rules that will enable them to say whether a particular set of starting numbers will produce 1 square, 2 squares, and so on.

Some of the rules could be written as follows:
- If all four starting numbers are the same, the differences will be the same in the first round of difference, i.e. 1 square.
- If two pairs of opposite starting numbers are the same, the differences will be the same in the first round, i.e. 1 square.
- If both pairs of opposite numbers are consecutive, the differences will be the same in the second round, i.e. 2 squares.
- If pairs of adjacent numbers are the same, the differences will be the same in the second round, i.e. 2 squares.
- If the four numbers are consecutive (working clockwise or anti-clockwise), the differences will be the same in the fourth round, i.e. 4 squares.

Encourage the children to use their rules to predict how many squares will be needed for particular sets of numbers.

Suggested questions:
- What do you notice?
- Why did you choose these starting numbers?
- What if the opposite starting numbers were consecutive/the same/had a difference of 2?
- What if the adjacent starting numbers were consecutive/the same/had a difference of 2?

Secret numbers (page 27)

☆ *Processes: trial and improvement, predict, record, reason, make decisions, estimate, compare, check*

Solutions:
$$35 \rightarrow 35 \div 25 = 1\cdot4$$
$$5\cdot4 \rightarrow 5\cdot4 \times 54 = 291\cdot6$$
$$\tfrac{6}{4} \rightarrow 6 \times 4 = 24 \quad 6 \div 4 = 1\tfrac{1}{2}$$
$$3\cdot7 \rightarrow 3\cdot7 \times 2\cdot7 = 9\cdot99 \text{ (or closer: for}$$
example, $3\cdot701 \times 2\cdot701 = 9\cdot996401$)

Suggested questions:
- How did you work that out?
- Should the next number you try be larger or smaller?

A dog's life (page 28)

☆ *Processes: reason, compare, look for pattern, trial and improvement, generalise*

Solutions:

	Human age (in years)	
Dog's age	Kate's rule	Tim's rule
1	7	–
2	14	23
3	21	27
4	28	31
5	35	35
6	42	39
7	49	43
8	56	47
9	63	51
10	70	55
11	77	59
12	84	63
13	91	67
14	98	71
15	105	75
16	112	79

Kate's rule most closely matches the table in the extension activity since, apart from the first year, the equivalent human age goes up in sevens. The rule for this table (apart from year 0) can be expressed as add 1, multiply by 7 and then subtract 2, or $7(x + 1) - 2$, which can be more simply written as multiply by 7 and add 5, i.e. $7x + 5$.

Suggested questions:
- What does this data mean?
- What patterns did you notice?
- Which rule is more suitable, and why?

Digit patterns (page 29)

☆ *Processes: look for pattern, generalise, predict, reason, explain*

Solutions showing patterns of units digits:

Multiples of 1 → 1…	for example 111111111111…
Multiples of 2 → 4862…	for example 486248624862…
Multiples of 3 → 9713…	for example 971397139713…
Multiples of 4 → 64…	for example 646464646464…
Multiples of 5 → 5…	for example 555555555555…
Multiples of 6 → 6…	for example 666666666666…
Multiples of 7 → 9317…	for example 931793179317…
Multiples of 8 → 4268…	for example 426842684268…
Multiples of 9 → 19…	for example 191919191919…

Related patterns are multiples of 2 and 8, 3 and 7.

Multiples of 11 → pattern is the same as multiples of 1
Multiples of 12 → pattern is the same as multiples of 2
Multiples of 13 → pattern is the same as multiples of 3, and so on.

So, multiples of 101 follow the same pattern as multiples of 1, multiples of 52 follow the same pattern as multiples of 2 and multiples of 88 follow the same pattern as multiples of 8.

Suggested questions:
- What patterns did you notice?
- Can you explain why this happens?

Solving problems

Shut that door! (page 30)

☆ *Processes: be systematic, look for pattern, generalise, check, compare, predict*

Discuss ways of working systematically, such as finding all the different ways where only one door is open, then where two doors are open, and so on.

Solutions:

1 door 2 ways
O
S

2 doors 4 ways
OO
OS SO
SS

3 doors 8 ways
OOO
OOS OSO SOO
OSS SSO SOS
SSS

4 doors 16 ways
OOOO
OOOS OOSO OSOO SOOO
SSOO SOOS SOSO OSOS OSSO OOSS
SSSO SSOS SOSS OSSS
SSSS

Therefore 5 doors would have 32 ways, and so on.

Suggested questions:
- What have you noticed about the number of ways?
- What patterns did you notice?
- For four doors, how many ways did you find with one/two/three/four doors open?

Let's go nuts! (page 31)

☆ *Processes: reason, simplify, visualise, look for pattern, explain, co-operate, test ideas, generalise*

This activity is based on a version of the ancient game 'Nim'. If a player is not allowed to move more than three squares up in a go, then the vital square to land on is the fourth square from the top, since this prevents your opponent from reaching the finish, and assures you of getting there in the next go. To be certain of reaching the fourth square, players should aim to be on the eighth square (from the top) at the end of their previous go. For longer tracks, this pattern continues in multiples of 4. Encourage the children to explore this by drawing longer tree trunks and numbering the squares to aid discussion.

Suggested questions:
- What patterns did you notice?
- What strategies did you use?
- Did the player who went first always win?
- What happens if we change the length of the trunk?

Bell-ringers: 1 and 2 (pages 32–33)

☆ *Processes: look for pattern, be systematic, record, compare, check*

There are six different rounds for three bells:

123, 132, 213, 231, 312, 321

These can be ordered to match the rule in many different ways, for example:

123	123	123	123
132	321	213	132
231	312	231	312
213	213	321	321
312	231	312	231
321	132	132	213

There are 24 different rounds for four bells:

1234	1243	1324	1342	1423	1432
2134	2143	2314	2341	2431	2413
3124	3142	3214	3241	3412	3421
4123	4132	4231	4213	4312	4321

The following is an example of how these can be ordered:

1234 → 1243 → 2143 → 2134 → 2314 → 2341 →
2431 → 2413 → 4213 → 4231 → 4321 → 4312 →
4132 → 4123 → 1423 → 1432 → 1342 → 1324 →
3124 → 3142 → 3412 → 3421 → 3241 → 3214

The joining of numbers can be called braiding. Patterns of the braids could be explored.

Suggested questions:
- Compare your results with a partner. What are the similarities and differences?
- When you joined up the same numbers in the list, what patterns did you notice?

Roll, roll, roll your dice (page 34)

☆ *Processes: visualise, reason, record, explain, be systematic, co-operate, trial and improvement*

There are two solutions, depending upon the dice used:

When the dice travels in a straight line, the numbers follow a repeating pattern.

Adjacent numbers along the route have differences of between one and four; most commonly the difference is two. It is impossible for there to be a difference of five since the only two numbers on the dice with a difference of five are 6 and 1 and these are on opposite faces.

Suggested questions/prompts:
- What patterns can you see in the numbers?
- Explain why there is never a difference of five between one number and the next.
- Is it possible to have three consecutive numbers in a row along the route: for example, 1, 2, 3, or 3, 4, 5? Explain your thinking.

Handling data

Find the key (page 35)

☆ *Processes: make decisions, co-operate, test ideas, reason, record, explain, simplify*

Allow children to make their own group decisions about how to find an answer to this question, and to choose appropriate ways of presenting this information to others. Different approaches could involve looking at text keyed into the computer, or at text in books and magazines.

Suggested questions:
- How well did your group work together?
- What went well? What problems did you have?
- If you were going to do this again, what changes would you make?

Finger angles (page 36)

☆ *Processes: predict, estimate, check, visualise, compare, test ideas, record*

This activity encourages the children to see the importance of gathering sufficient information before generalising or making a definite statement. The use of databases can assist children in sorting the data to find out whether a person with longer fingers has a larger finger angle. The children could explore lengths and angles for other fingers, and could also investigate whether one hand's angles differ from the other hand.

Suggested questions:
- Was your prediction correct?
- Have you found out enough information to be sure of your answer to the question?
- How did the databases help you?

Measures, shape and space

Palindromic times (page 37)

☆ *Processes: predict, make decisions, be systematic, record, test ideas, check*

There are 57 different palindromic times in a 12-hour period. These include six times in each of the hours between 1:00 and 9:59, and one time during each of the hours between 10:00 and 12:59.

Listing solutions can help the children to see patterns, for example:

1:01	1:11	1:21	1:31	1:41	1:51
2:02	2:12	2:22	2:32	2:42	2:52...
9:09	9:19	9:29	9:39	9:49	9:59
10:01					
11:11					
12:21					

If a 12-hour clock includes a zero in front of single-digit hours (for example, 04:40), then there are eight solutions, as follows:

01:10 02:20 03:30 04:40 05:50
10:01
11:11
12:21

For reference, in a 24-hour period with a standard four-digit 24-hour clock, there are 16 solutions:

01:10 02:20 03:30 04:40 05:50 10:01 11:11 12:21
13:31 14:41 15:51 20:02 21:12 22:22 23:32 00:00

Suggested questions:
● What strategies did you use to find the times?
● How many have you found?
● How many more do you predict there will be?
● How could you arrange the times to check whether you have missed any?

What's my card? (page 38)
☆ *Processes: explain, co-operate, compare, record, visualise*

This activity focuses attention on describing diagrams accurately and explaining where two lines and a dot lie in relation to one another. Encourage the children to use specific language, such as the words in the box on the activity sheet.

Suggested questions:
● In what way is this card different from this one?
● How could you describe this card?
● Does your description only fit this card, or could it describe one of the other cards too?

One man went to mow... (page 39)
☆ *Processes: look for pattern, reason, visualise, explain, compare, test ideas*

The children should notice that all the routes around the lawn have the same length (not including the walk back to the start) – 49 m if counted from the middle of one square to the middle of the next. There are several routes where the walk back is only 1 m, such as the one shown here.

Suggested questions:
● What patterns have you noticed?
● What if you tried a different-sized rectangular lawn?

The Dark Ages (page 40)
☆ *Processes: make decisions, explain, compare, co-operate, check*

Remind the children of units of time: 60 seconds = 1 minute, 60 minutes = 1 hour, 24 hours = 1 day, 7 days = 1 week, 365 days = 1 year. The ages on the activity sheet are:

400 million seconds = 12 years, 35 weeks, 4 days, 15 hours, 6 minutes and 40 seconds

5 million minutes = 9 years, 26 weeks, 5 days, 5 hours and 20 minutes

80 000 hours = 9 years, 6 weeks, 6 days and 8 hours

4000 days = 10 years and 50 weeks

500 weeks = 9 years, 30 weeks and 5 days

100 months = 8 years and 4 months

Suggested questions:
● How did you work that out?
● What decisions did you make?
● How close is your estimate?
● Did you think about leap years?
● Who is going to have their 3500-day birthday next?

A lengthy challenge (page 41)
☆ *Processes: estimate, check, visualise, record, co-operate, predict, reason, compare*

Estimating is a valuable using and applying skill. This activity encourages the children to estimate a range of classroom distances and other measurements of length.

Suggested questions:
● How good were your estimates?
● Did you get better each time you estimated?

Time to reflect (page 42)
☆ *Processes: visualise, generalise, look for pattern, explain, co-operate, test ideas*

Each time on an analogue clock will have a related reflected time: for example, 9:00 and 3:00. For 12:00 and 6:00, the time and its reflection are the same. The children should notice that if a time and its reflection are added together, they total 12:00 (for example, 5:15 + 6:45) or 24:00 (for example, 11:15 + 12:45). Listing the times in order can help children to see the patterns.

Suggested questions:
● What patterns have you noticed?
● Does every time have a different reflection time?
● What rule could you use to find the reflection time?

Trying tiles (page 43)
☆ *Processes: visualise, look for pattern, make decisions, predict, co-operate, test ideas, record*

Solutions:

1	1	1	1
1	1	1	1
1	1	1	1
1	1	1	1

3	4	3	4
3	4	3	4
3	4	3	4
3	4	3	4

4	1	4	1
1	4	1	4
4	1	4	1
1	4	1	4

3	1	3	1
1	3	1	3
3	1	3	1
1	3	1	3

2	1	2	1
3	4	3	4
2	1	2	1
3	4	3	4

4	2	4	2
4	2	4	2
4	2	4	2
4	2	4	2

Suggested questions:
● What patterns have you made?
● What is special about the numbers?
● Is your pattern symmetrical?

Diagonal cuts (page 44)

☆ *Processes: look for pattern, generalise, predict, record, reason, compare, ask own questions*

When looking for rules and generalising, the children might find it useful to arrange all the rectangles they have explored in sets, according to whether there is an even or odd number of rows.

- The children should notice that for all rectangles with 1 row or column, every square will be cut through.
- Square grids can produce odd numbers: for example, $3 \times 3 \rightarrow 3$.

Patterns can be seen as follows:

$$2 \times 3 \rightarrow 4$$
$$2 \times 4 \rightarrow 4$$
$$2 \times 5 \rightarrow 6$$
$$2 \times 6 \rightarrow 6$$
$$2 \times 7 \rightarrow 8$$
$$2 \times 8 \rightarrow 8 \text{ and so on}$$
$$3 \times 4 \rightarrow 6$$
$$3 \times 5 \rightarrow 7$$
$$3 \times 6 \rightarrow 6$$
$$3 \times 7 \rightarrow 9$$
$$3 \times 8 \rightarrow 10$$
$$3 \times 9 \rightarrow 9 \text{ and so on}$$

Encourage the children to begin to make predictions about the number of cut-through squares that will be produced by a particular rectangle they have drawn.

Suggested questions:

- What other patterns have you noticed?
- Can you write what you have found in a list?
- How can you use what you have found to make predictions about other rectangles?

Friday the 13th (page 45)

☆ *Processes: generalise, test ideas, look for pattern, reason, explain, compare*

Solutions:

There is one Friday the 13th in the year shown, in May.

1st January = Sunday	12th January = Thursday
27th January = Friday	9th February = Thursday
16th July = Sunday	15th December = Friday

January and October will have a Friday the 13th. (This can be found by looking at the Thursday dates of the previous year).

The children may realise that a Friday the 13th occurs in any month that begins on a Sunday. Every year has at least one Friday the 13th, most have two and sometimes there are three (2009 is the next year that will have three Friday the 13ths).

Suggested questions:

- Compare the day of the week of any date this year with the day of the week it will fall on next year. What do you notice?
- What effect does a leap year have?

Overground map (page 46)

☆ *Processes: visualise, record, test ideas, simplify*

This activity allows children to make their own decisions about ways to record position and movements that are possible about the school building.

Once the children have completed their maps, ask them to compare approaches and to say which they prefer, and why.

Suggested questions:

- On the map shown here, can you walk straight from the playground to the entrance?
- What places can be reached from Class 3/4G?
- Is your map the same as your partner's?

Shapes shifters: 1 and 2 (pages 47–48)

☆ *Processes: visualise, record, trial and improvement, reason, compare, test ideas*

Some children may find it easier to work with cardboard shapes.

Solutions:

1. Patterns can take a variety of forms, for example:

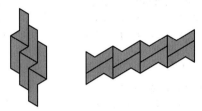

2. Patterns with reflective symmetry, such as the one below, can be made only when some of the pieces are turned over.

3. Six pieces can be used to make a star as shown below.

4. Three pieces can be joined to make a triangle with a hole in, or a closed shape that is a nonagon.

Suggested questions:

- What patterns have you made?
- Did you find it difficult to visualise?
- What difficulties did you have in drawing these patterns?

Fantastic fractions

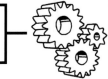

- **Use these digits:** 2 3 4 5

1. Write all the fractions you can make using the digits above.
   Do not use the same digit twice in a fraction.
   Some fractions could be **improper fractions** (greater than 1).

$\frac{2}{3}$ $\frac{5}{4}$

2. Now arrange your fractions on this grid.
   Fractions in the same row should have the
   same **denominator**. Fractions in the same
   column should have the same **numerator**.

   Some boxes will be empty.

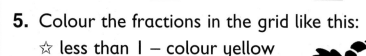

3. How many boxes are empty? _____

4. Which fraction is:

   (a) smallest? ☐ **(b)** largest? ☐

5. Colour the fractions in the grid like this:
   ☆ less than 1 – colour yellow
   ☆ greater than 1 – colour green

   What patterns do you notice?

6. Which row of fractions has the greatest total? _____

- **Explore four other digits in the same way. Will you always have the same number of fractions coloured yellow and green? Can you explain why?**

Teachers' note Revise the meaning of 'numerator' (top number), 'denominator' (bottom number) and 'improper fraction'. Explain that for this activity the numerator and denominator should have only one digit (for example, $\frac{2}{5}$ may be used but $\frac{25}{3}$ may not). Arranging the fractions systematically in the grid helps the children to see any they have missed. Some children may require help in adding the fractions. Remind them that when the denominator is the same we can simply add the numerators.

**Developing Numeracy
Using & Applying Maths
Year 5
© A & C BLACK**

14

Reason, explain and make predictions

This grid shows numbers in Chinese from ☐1 to ☐100. Some of the numbers are missing.

You need a 100-square.

一	二	三	四	五	六	七		九	十
十一	十二	十三		十五	十六		十八	十九	二十
二十一	二十二			二十五	二十六	二十七		二十九	
三十一	三十二		三十四	三十五		三十七	三十八		四十
四十一		四十三	四十四	四十五		四十七	四十八	四十九	五十
	五十二	五十三		五十五		五十七	五十八	五十九	六十
六十一	六十二		六十四	六十五	六十六		六十八	六十九	
七十一	七十二	七十三	七十四		七十六	七十七	七十八		
八十一		八十三	八十四		八十六	八十七	八十八	八十九	九十
九十一	九十二	九十三		九十五	九十六		九十八		一百

- **Compare the Chinese numbers with the numbers in a 100-square. Work out how to write the missing Chinese numbers and fill them in.**
- **Now write these numbers in Chinese:**

  101 _____   123 _____   602 _____   815 _____

- **Write four other numbers in figures and in Chinese.**

  _____   _____   _____   _____

- **Write an explanation of how to write Chinese numbers up to 99 using only the first ten symbols.**

Teachers' note This activity helps the children begin to appreciate systems of place value. Encourage them to discuss the patterns they notice with a partner, and to explain the patterns verbally and in writing. Being able to communicate findings is an important aspect of using and applying skills and the children should be encouraged to compare explanations and to make comments about which they feel is most effective.

**Developing Numeracy
Using & Applying Maths
Year 5
© A & C BLACK**

Reason and make decisions

Tom sends Kuldip a message in code, using percentages.

- **Crack the code to work out the message.**

The first 40% of the word WATER	WA
The middle 50% of the word WITH	_____
The last 25% of the word HALF	_____
The first 25% of the word ORNAMENT	_____
The first 20% of the word MEANDERING	_____

Write the message here.

WA _____
_____

- **Work out Kuldip's reply.**

The last 20% of the word BELOW	_____
The last 80% of the word THERE	_____
The middle 50% of the word BABE	_____
The first 25% of the word OUTSIDER	_____
The last 50% of the word PETS	_____

_____
_____ ?

- **Now make up Tom's answer in code. Think carefully about the number of letters in the words you use.**

- **Check your code. Then give it to a partner to solve.**

Now try this!

- **Write a new message in code. Use three-letter words and these percentages:** | 100% | $33\frac{1}{3}$% | $66\frac{2}{3}$% |

Teachers' note Begin the lesson by revising simple percentages of numbers and the links between such percentages and their equivalent fractions. Write on the board 10% = $\frac{1}{10}$, 25% = $\frac{1}{4}$, 20% = $\frac{1}{5}$, and so on. Demonstrate several examples of how to crack the code (see page 7). When the children make up their own codes, they might find it useful to have a list of ten-letter words on the board.

**Developing Numeracy
Using & Applying Maths
Year 5
© A & C BLACK**

Trainspotting

☆ Choose a number from 2 to 12. Write the first ten multiples of that number in the windows of a train.

☆ Add the digits of each multiple. Write the sum in the wheel below.

You need two copies of this sheet.

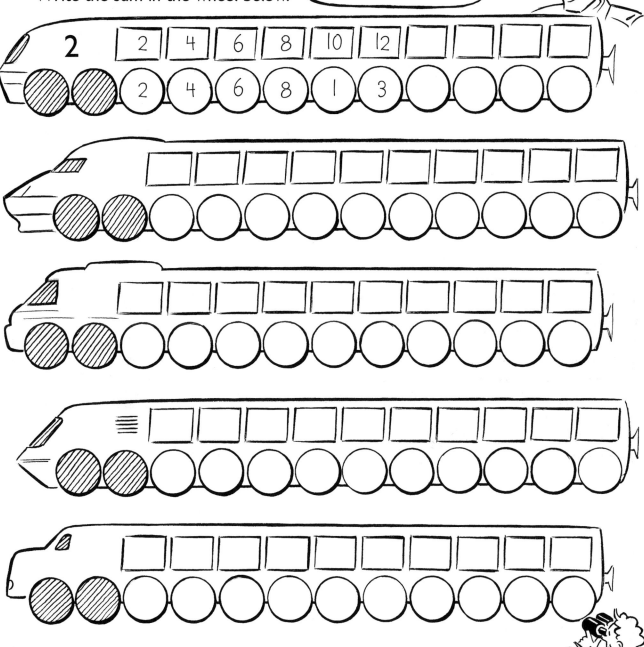

• **Look for patterns in the sums of the digits.**

Talk to a partner about what you notice.

• **Write rules for how you can recognise some multiples by adding the digits.**

Teachers' note Give each child two copies of the sheet and suggest that each pair ensures they cover all the numbers from 2 to 12 between them. For the extension activity, encourage the children to devise clear rules as to how to recognise multiples of 3, 6 and 9. These could be written on large pieces of paper and displayed. The knowledge gained in this activity can help the children to provide explanations for the patterns they discover on page 18.

Developing Numeracy Using & Applying Maths Year 5 © A & C BLACK

Making chains

Look for patterns

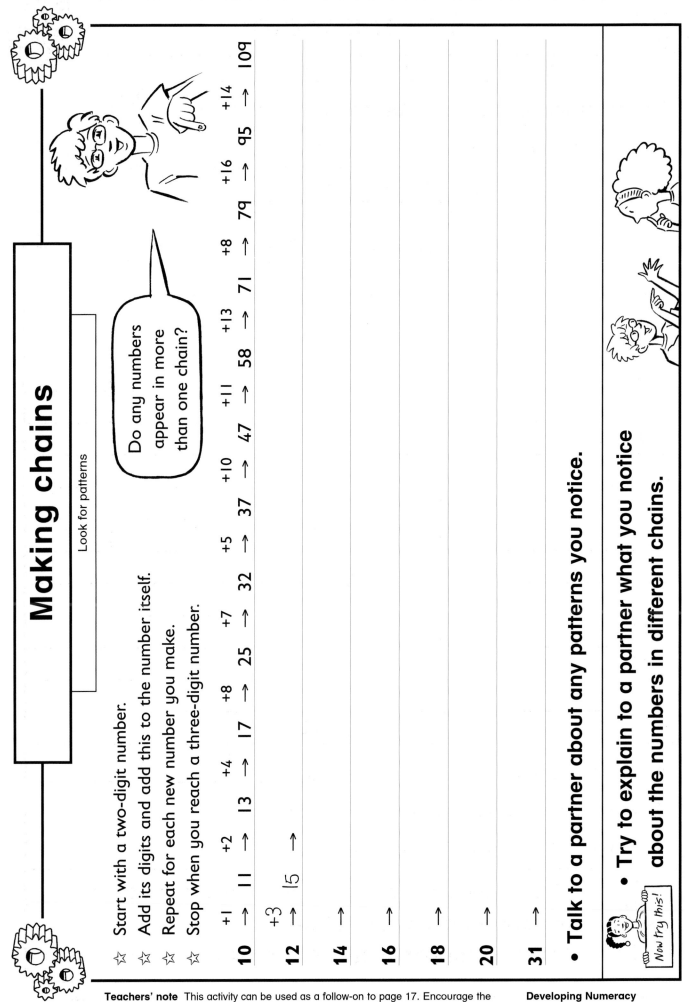

☆ Start with a two-digit number.

☆ Add its digits and add this to the number itself.

☆ Repeat for each new number you make.

☆ Stop when you reach a three-digit number.

Do any numbers appear in more than one chain?

10 → 11 +2→ 13 +4→ 17 +8→ 25 +7→ 32 +5→ 37 +10→ 47 +11→ 58 +13→ 71 +8→ 79 +16→ 95 +14→ 109
+1

12 +3→ 15 →

14 →

16 →

18 →

20 →

31 →

• Talk to a partner about any patterns you notice.

Now try this!

• Try to explain to a partner what you notice about the numbers in different chains.

Teachers' note This activity can be used as a follow-on to page 17. Encourage the children to discuss any patterns they notice in the chains: for example, whether they recognise numbers in a chain as multiples of a particular number (such as 3 or 9). As a further extension, the children could consider what would happen if the total of the digits was subtracted from, rather than added to, a two-digit number.

Developing Numeracy
Using & Applying Maths
Year 5
© A & C BLACK

18

The fun factor

The number ⬚6 **has four factors:** ⬚1 ⬚2 ⬚3 ⬚6

1. Complete the chart for each number from **1** to **30**.

Check your answers with a partner.

Number	Factors	Number of factors	Number	Factors	Number of factors
1			16		
2			17		
3			18		
4			19		
5			20		
6	1, 2, 3, 6	4	21		
7			22		
8			23		
9			24		
10			25		
11			26		
12			27		
13			28		
14			29		
15			30		

2. Which numbers have exactly three factors? _____

3. What is the most common number of factors? _____

4. Which number less than 30 has the most factors? _____

- **List all the numbers that have an odd number of factors. What do you notice?**
- **Talk to a partner about other patterns you see.**

Teachers' note Begin the lesson by revising the word 'factor' and discussing strategies for finding pairs of factors. Remind the children that every number has the factors 1 and itself. Some children may find it useful to have a list of the multiplication tables facts on the board. Further discussion of square numbers could take place, and numbers above 30 could also be explored.

Developing Numeracy
Using & Applying Maths
Year 5
© A & C BLACK

What's going on?

You need a calculator.

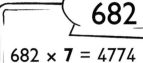

682

☆ Write any three-digit number.

☆ Multiply this number by 7.

☆ Multiply your answer by 11.

☆ Multiply your new answer by 13.

$682 \times 7 = 4774$

$4774 \times 11 = 52\,514$

$52\,514 \times 13 = $ _____

• **Write the final answer.**

What do you notice? _____

_____

• **Try this for other three-digit numbers.**

• **Try to explain to a partner why this works.**

• **Start with a two-digit number. What happens when you follow the same instructions? Why does this work?**

Teachers' note To help the children see why digits are repeated, encourage them to think of the multiplications as one whole step and find how many they have multiplied by altogether, i.e. 7 × 11 × 13 (1001). Once this number has been found, the children could choose further two- or three- digit numbers and multiply them mentally by this number (by 1000 and then by 1). This might help them to see why the pattern occurs.

Developing Numeracy
Using & Applying Maths
Year 5
© A & C BLACK

20

Yo-ho-ho!

Reason, explain and co-operate with others

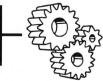

Gold coins

Pegleg Peggy and Wooden-eye Will are pirates. Each has fewer than ten gold coins.

If Peggy gave Will one of her coins, Will would have twice as many coins as Peggy.

But if Will gave Peggy one of his coins, they would both have the same number of coins.

• **How many coins did they each start with?**

Gold earrings

Captain Jake and Dirty Dan are pirates. Each has fewer than ten gold earrings.

If Jake gave Dan one of his earrings, Dan would have twice as many earrings as Jake.

But if Dan gave Jake one of his earrings, Jake would have one earring more than Dan.

• **How many earrings did they each start with?**

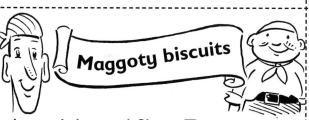

Maggoty biscuits

Long John and Short Tim are pirates. Each has fewer than ten maggoty biscuits.

If John gave Tim two of his biscuits, Tim would have twice as many biscuits as John.

But if Tim gave John two of his biscuits, John would have twice as many biscuits as Tim.

• **How many biscuits did they each start with?**

Treasure maps

Crazy Jack and Manic Mary are pirates. Each has fewer than ten treasure maps.

If Jack gave Mary three of his maps, Mary would have twice as many maps as Jack.

But if Jack gave Mary only one of his maps, they would both have the same number of maps.

• **How many maps did they each start with?**

Teachers' note Begin the lesson by talking to the class about rules for working in a group (see page 8). In groups of three or four, the children should discuss a puzzle and write a group answer to it. Cards could be allocated to groups, or groups could tackle the puzzle or puzzles of their choice. See page 8 for solutions. Discuss how the children might use practical equipment or draw the situation on paper to help them solve the problems.

**Developing Numeracy
Using & Applying Maths
Year 5
© A & C BLACK**

Billy's Fizz Factory

Billy is weighing fizz powder to add to his Fizz Ball Wizard sweets.

He uses balance scales, but he only has **10 kg** and **7 kg** weights.

To weigh out **1 kg** of fizz, he does this:

1 kg of fizz

• **Show how he could weigh other amounts of fizz up to** $\boxed{20\,kg}$.

Weight	Left pan	Right pan
1 kg	7 + 7 + 7	10 + 10 + fizz

Now try this!

• **Try other amounts to** $\boxed{50\,kg}$ **. Do you think it is possible to weigh out all whole number amounts?**

Teachers' note Explain that a pan can contain one type of weight, both types, or no weight: for example, to weigh 17 kg you could put the fizz in one pan and a 10 kg and a 7 kg weight in the other. Ask the children to look for patterns in the numbers and to describe the patterns to a partner. Encourage children who have not worked systematically to rewrite their table in order, starting with 1 kg, then 2 kg, and so on. This will enable them to see patterns more clearly.

**Developing Numeracy
Using & Applying Maths
Year 5
© A & C BLACK**

Multiple choice

Make predictions, reason and test your ideas

- **Predict** **how many numbers from 1 to 100 are:**

multiples of 5	20	multiples of 10	
multiples of 4		multiples of 2	
multiples of 3		multiples of 8	
multiples of 7		multiples of 6	
multiples of 1		multiples of 9	

- **How did you make your predictions? Talk to a partner.**

- **Now check your predictions. Write the correct answers here.**

multiples of 5		multiples of 10	
multiples of 4		multiples of 2	
multiples of 3		multiples of 8	
multiples of 7		multiples of 6	
multiples of 1		multiples of 9	

- **Write about any patterns you notice. Do the patterns work for all the multiples? Try to explain why these patterns happen.**

_____

_____

_____

_____

- **Predict how many numbers from 1 to 300 are multiples of 15. Use what you have discovered.**

- **Now check your prediction and write the answer.**

- **Choose other multiples and predict how many there are from 1 to 300.**

Now try this!

Teachers' note Adults might find this activity relatively simple, but children often need to work through these ideas and test them before they are convinced of the patterns. Limit the amount of predicting time to ensure that the children are not actually counting. Provide hundred squares so that the children can find and count the multiples when checking their predictions.

Developing Numeracy
Using & Applying Maths
Year 5
© A & C BLACK

Calculating creatures

On some phones, the buttons show numbers **and** letters.

If each letter stands for a digit, these three-digit numbers can be made:

a n t = 268

f l y = 359

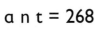

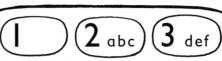

- **Here are some three-letter creatures. Write their numbers.**

dog _364_	bat _____	ram _____	bee _____	emu _____	pig _____
rat _____	yak _____	hen _____	sow _____	elk _____	fox _____
cow _____	hog _____	ewe _____	eel _____	gnu _____	kid _____

- **Choose two creatures and find their total.**
  Try to make a real word for this total.

- **Try other pairs of creatures. Find as many real words as you can.**

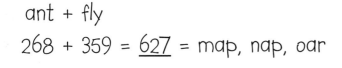

Some totals will not make real words.

ant + fly

268 + 359 = _627_ = map, nap, oar

Now try this!

- **Did you give up on any calculation part-way through because you realised it would not work? Why?**

Teachers' note This activity has been designed to encourage the children to use trial and improvement strategies and then to begin to reason about which calculations are unlikely to make real words: for example, those with a total above 1000, since there are no letters representing the digit 1. The children will need to continue recording their calculations and words on a separate piece of paper.

Developing Numeracy
Using & Applying Maths
Year 5
© A & C BLACK

Daffodil dilemma

Reason, record information and make predictions

Class 5 are planting bulbs. Every daffodil bulb they plant will split into two bulbs in a year's time. Each following year, every bulb will split into two again, and so on.

You need a calculator.

- **The class plant ten bulbs. If no bulbs die, how many years will it take to produce more than** one million **bulbs?**
- **Predict the answer, then work it out.**

My prediction

_____ years

- **Record your working out here.**

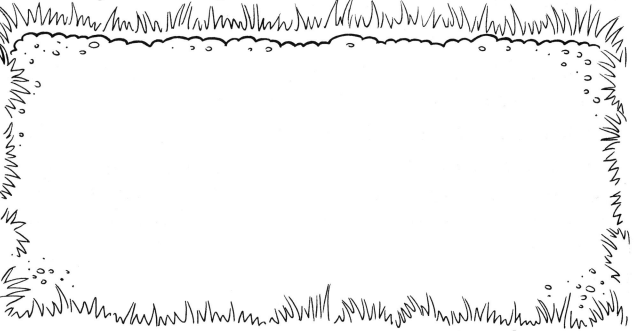

- **How many years would it take if the class planted:**

20 bulbs? _____ years   40 bulbs? _____ years   160 bulbs? _____ years

Now try this!

- **Imagine** 10% **of the bulbs die each year. Estimate how many years it will take to reach one million bulbs, if the class plant:**

10 bulbs _____ years   100 bulbs _____ years

- **Use a calculator to work out the answers.**

Teachers' note Allow children the opportunity to decide how best to set out their work. Some may make random jottings; others might choose to make a list or table. Once solutions have been found, compare the different recording methods and discuss which were most effective in avoiding mistakes, and which can now most easily be understood by other people. Demonstrate how information in a table shows patterns more clearly and can be easily understood by others.

**Developing Numeracy
Using & Applying Maths
Year 5
© A & C BLACK**

25

Square subtractions

☆ Choose four numbers from **1** to **9**. Write them at the corners of a large square.

☆ Find the difference between adjacent numbers. Write it at the **mid-point**.

☆ Join the mid-points to make a new square.

☆ Continue until the differences are the same.

Here, **three** squares are drawn.

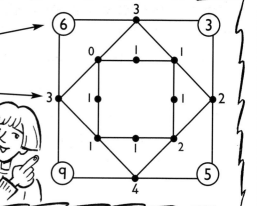

• **Follow the instructions for different sets of numbers.**

Investigate how many squares you need each time.

You can use a number more than once.

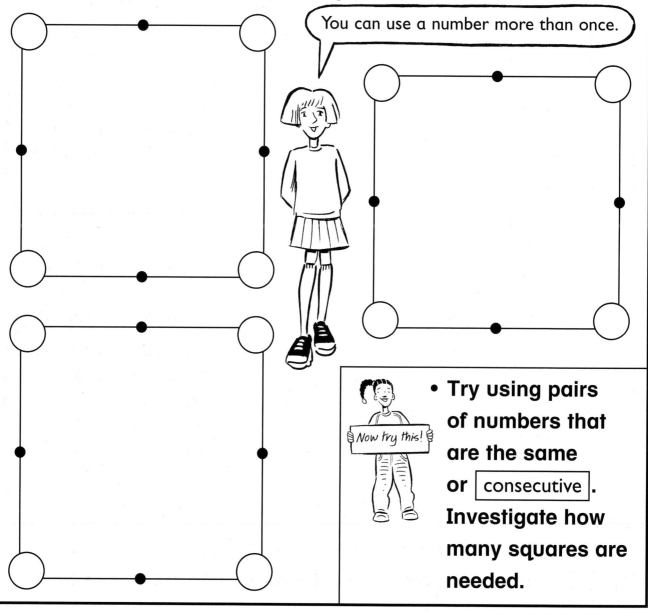

Now try this!

• **Try using pairs of numbers that are the same or** consecutive **. Investigate how many squares are needed.**

Teachers' note First complete several examples of these squares as a class, explaining the terms 'mid-point' and 'adjacent'. For the extension activity, the children could work in pairs. Provide squared paper and explain that they should try pairs of the same or consecutive numbers in both adjacent and diagonally opposite positions. Encourage them to devise rules that show which starting numbers will produce 1, 2, 3, 4, 5 or 6 squares (see page 9).

Developing Numeracy
Using & Applying Maths
Year 5
© A & C BLACK

26

Secret numbers

- ## You need a calculator.

A secret number is describing itself. What is it?

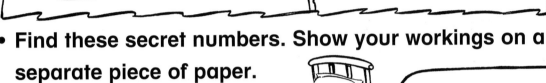

> I am a whole number. When you multiply me by the number that is 3 less than me, you get the answer 340.

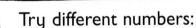

Try different numbers:
10 × 7 = 70   too low
15 × 12 = 180 too low
20 × 17 = 340 ✔
So the secret number is **20**.

- ## Find these secret numbers. Show your workings on a separate piece of paper.

> I am a whole number. When you divide me by the number that is 10 less than me, you get the answer 1·4.

> I am a decimal number. When you multiply me by the number that is ten times greater than me, you get the answer 291·6.

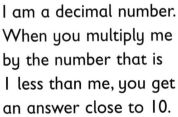

> I am a fraction greater than $\frac{1}{2}$. When you multiply my numerator by my denominator, you get 24. When you divide my numerator by my denominator, you get $1\frac{1}{2}$.

> I am a decimal number. When you multiply me by the number that is 1 less than me, you get an answer close to 10.

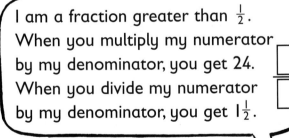

- ## Make up your own number riddles for a partner to solve. Make sure you know the correct answers.

Teachers' note Ensure that the children understand what is being asked. Encourage them to choose a number to test, see whether the answer is too large or too small, and then modify their next choice of number accordingly. In the example at the top of the page, the number 10 produces an answer that is too small and so a larger number should be chosen to test next. Explain that the idea is to try to zoom in closer to the answer each time.

**Developing Numeracy
Using & Applying Maths
Year 5
© A & C BLACK**

A dog's life

Reason and make comparisons

Here are two opinions about how to compare a dog's age with a human age.

Kate

If you multiply a dog's age by 7, you get its equivalent human age.

Tim

No, you should multiply a dog's age by 4 years and add 15 (but this doesn't work for the first year).

- **Find the equivalent human age for dogs aged up to 16 years. Use Kate's rule and then Tim's rule.**

Dog's age	Human age (in years)	
	Kate's rule	Tim's rule
1	7	——
2		
3		
4		
5		
6		
7		
8		
9		
10		
11		
12		
13		
14		
15		
16		

- **Talk to a partner about these questions:**

What are some of the differences between the human ages found using Kate's and Tim's rules?

For which dog age do both rules give the same human age?

Which rule do you think is more suitable, and why?

 Now try this!

- **Whose rule most closely matches the number pattern in this table?** _____

Dog's age	1	2	3	4	5	6	7	8	9
Human age	12	19	26	33	40	47	54	61	68

- **Find a rule that matches the ages in this table.**

Teachers' note Ensure that the children understand the principle of human equivalent ages: explain that dogs do not live as long as humans, and that we can use a calculation to see whereabouts in their life they are in equivalent human terms. Encourage discussion and co-operation in each pair and invite them to report back to others in the class.

Developing Numeracy
Using & Applying Maths
Year 5
© A & C BLACK

Look for patterns and generalise

☆ Start with a single-digit number.   8

☆ Multiply it by itself. $8 \times 8 = 64$

☆ Multiply the units digit of the answer by the original number. $4 \times 8 = 32$

☆ Multiply the units digit of the answer by the original number. $2 \times 8 = 16$

☆ Keep going like this until you see a pattern. $6 \times 8 = 48$

                                                                     $8 \times 8 = 64$

• **Choose different single-digit numbers. Follow the instructions.**

• **Look at the units digits of the answers. Talk to a partner about the patterns you see. Try to explain why they happen.**

Are any patterns the reverse of others?

Now try this!

• **What happens if you start with the number** | 11 |**?**

• **Investigate other numbers. Use this to predict the pattern for these numbers:** | 101 | | 52 | | 88 |

You need a calculator.

Teachers' note Once the children have investigated and spotted patterns in the units digits of the answers, it is important that they are given an opportunity to discuss and suggest reasons and to begin to make generalisations. By encouraging the children to explore other numbers with a calculator, the extension activity helps them to see that any number with a particular units digit will follow the same pattern (for example, 2, 12 and 32 all follow the same pattern).

Developing Numeracy
Using & Applying Maths
Year 5
© A & C BLACK

Shut that door!

In a toilet block, there are three doors in a row.
Each door can be open or shut.

This arrangement is:

SOS!

Shut Open Shut
or **SOS**

- **Record all the different arrangements for the doors.**
  Use the letters [S] **and** [O].

SOS   SSO

- **In a different toilet block, there are** [four] **doors in a row.**
- **Record all the different arrangements.**

Now try this!

- **Predict the number of arrangements for:**

  five doors [ ]   **six** doors [ ]   **seven** doors [ ]

Teachers' note Discuss ways of working systematically, such as finding all the different arrangements where only one door is open, then where two doors are open, and so on. Counting the number of different solutions of each type can help the children to identify any missing solutions. See page 10 for more information on this pattern.

Developing Numeracy
Using & Applying Maths
Year 5
© A & C BLACK

Let's go nuts!

Simplify and reason

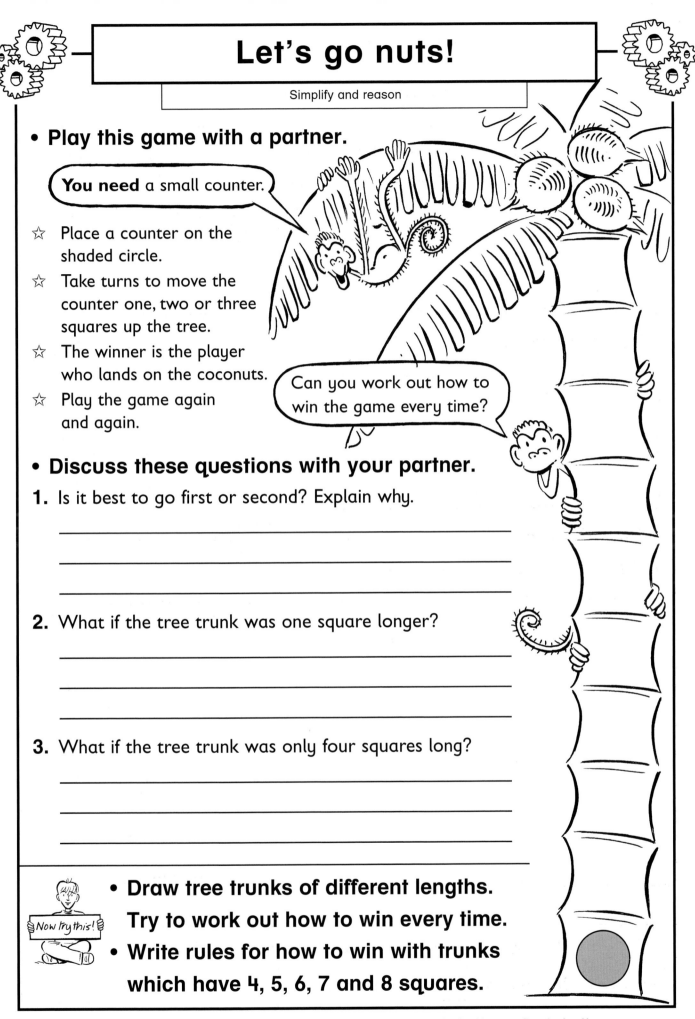

- **Play this game with a partner.**

  You need a small counter.

  ☆ Place a counter on the shaded circle.
  ☆ Take turns to move the counter one, two or three squares up the tree.
  ☆ The winner is the player who lands on the coconuts.
  ☆ Play the game again and again.

  Can you work out how to win the game every time?

- **Discuss these questions with your partner.**

1. Is it best to go first or second? Explain why.

   _____

   _____

   _____

2. What if the tree trunk was one square longer?

   _____

   _____

   _____

3. What if the tree trunk was only four squares long?

   _____

   _____

   _____

Now try this!

- **Draw tree trunks of different lengths. Try to work out how to win every time.**
- **Write rules for how to win with trunks which have 4, 5, 6, 7 and 8 squares.**

Teachers' note Give each pair one copy of the sheet. A way of finding winning strategies for this game is to simplify it by considering tracks which have 4, 5, 6, 7 and 8 squares and examining what a player must do in each situation. This can help the children to focus on the importance of having the counter on a particular square by the end of their go. It can help if the squares are numbered from the top of the tree downwards (for example, 1 to 10 from top to bottom in the tree trunk shown).

**Developing Numeracy
Using & Applying Maths
Year 5
© A & C BLACK**

Bell-ringers: 1

Look for patterns and be systematic

Three bell-ringers ring a bell each.

They ring the bells in different orders.

They always start with this order:

1 2 3   *This is called a **round**.*

Each bell is rung once in each round.

- **Write all the different rounds for** ⬚three⬚ **bells.**

  1   2   3   _____   _____

  _____

Bell-ringers play all the rounds in a particular order.

They use this **rule**:

In each round the order stays the same as the last, apart from two ringers who switch.

- **Write all the rounds in order to match the rule above.**

  Find four different ways that this can be done.

1 2 3	1 2 3	1 2 3	1 2 3
1 3 2			

Now try this!

- **In each list above, draw lines to join up the same numbers. Use three different-coloured pencils.**
- **What patterns do you notice?**

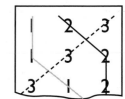

Teachers' note Ensure the children understand that no two rounds in the list should be the same. When finding all the permutations, encourage the children to count the number of ways they have written that start with each number (they should find two ways for each number). Check they understand that when writing the permutations in order according to the rule, one number should stay in the same position as the line above, and the other two numbers should switch places.

**Developing Numeracy
Using & Applying Maths
Year 5
© A & C BLACK**

Four bell-ringers ring a bell each.

They ring the bells in different orders.

They always start with this order:

1   2   3   4   This is called a **round**.

Each bell is rung once in each round.

- **Write the 24 different rounds for** four **bells.**

1	2	3	4

1 2 3 4   1 2 4 3   1 3 2 4

_____   _____   _____

_____   _____   _____

_____   _____   _____

_____   _____   _____

_____   _____   _____

Bell-ringers play all the rounds in a
particular order. They use this **rule**:

In each round the order stays the same,
apart from two ringers who switch.

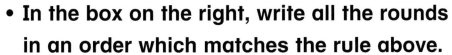

- **In the box on the right, write all the rounds**
  in an order which matches the rule above.

Now try this!

- **In your list, draw lines**
  to join up the same
  numbers. Use three
  different-coloured pencils.

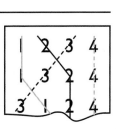

- **What patterns do you notice?**

Teachers' note When finding all the permutations, encourage the children to count the number of
ways they have written that start with each number (they should find six ways for each number).
Ensure the children understand that when writing the permutations in order according to the rule, two
numbers should stay in the same position as the line above and the other two numbers should
switch places. Suggest that they cross each round off their original list so that no two are repeated.

Developing Numeracy
Using & Applying Maths
Year 5
© A & C BLACK

Roll, roll, roll your dice

You need a dice.

☆ Place a dice on START so that the number on the **top** of the dice matches the number on the square.

☆ Now carefully roll the dice over onto its side.

☆ Does the number on the **top** of the dice match the number on the new square? If not, roll the dice back and try a different direction.

☆ Keep rolling the dice like this and try to reach FINISH. Use a pencil to mark the route as you go.

FINISH

1	2	3	2	4	5	3	2	4	5
1	5	6	1	4	6	3	1	1	6
4	3	5	5	3	5	4	2	3	5
6	5	3	6	1	START 6	4	6	3	1
6	3	2	2	4	2	2	6	6	4
2	1	4	6	4	1	3	3	5	5
1	5	4	2	3	5	1	4	6	3
5	3	2	4	5	3	2	1	4	5

Now try this!

- **Look for patterns in the numbers along your route.**
- **Now find the difference between each number and the next.**

What is the most common difference?

Do any numbers have a difference of five or zero? Why might this be?

Teachers' note This activity requires careful perseverance and some children will find it difficult. Demonstrate how to gently roll the dice over onto an adjacent face to land on a new square, and emphasise the importance of working slowly and methodically, recording each step as they go. Encourage discussion about why some routes are not possible: for example, 'Why is it not possible to roll from 6 to 1 or from 3 to 4?'

**Developing Numeracy
Using & Applying Maths
Year 5
© A & C BLACK**

Find the key

Make decisions, co-operate and test your ideas

- **Work in a small group.**
  Discuss how you could find out
  the answer to this question:

  *Which **letter key** on a computer keyboard is pressed most often?*

- **Make a list of what you are going to do.**

How we plan to find out the information (who will do what?)
What resources we will need

- **Now follow your plan. Write what you find out.**

  _____

  _____

  _____

- **Do you think you have enough information to answer the question? Explain your thinking.**

  _____

  _____

  _____

Now try this!

- **Find out whether the space bar is pressed more often than the letter key of your answer.**

Teachers' note This activity allows the children to be in charge of their own planning and to make decisions about how to investigate fairly. Encourage groups to compare and discuss the different approaches they choose. The children could be asked to represent their findings in charts or graphs to show their results clearly for others to see. Discuss differences between their results, and the reasons behind these.

Developing Numeracy
Using & Applying Maths
Year 5
© A & C BLACK

Finger angles

Make predictions, estimate and check

Stretch out your fingers as far as you can. You are going to investigate the angles between your fingers.

1. Do you think that people with longer

fingers will have larger angles?

Circle your prediction.

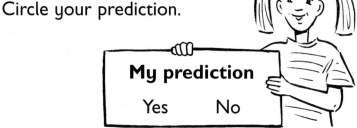

My prediction

Yes   No

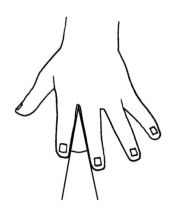

2. (a) Estimate the length of your middle finger.

_____

(b) Now measure to check your estimate.

_____

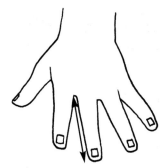

3. (a) Estimate the angle between your first two fingers.

_____

(b) Now measure to check your estimate.

_____

You need a protractor.

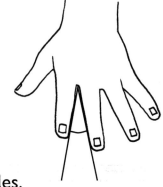

4. Find out about other people's finger lengths and angles.

Do you think your prediction was correct?

• **Collect and record other people's measurements. Choose your own way of recording.**

Teachers' note Begin the lesson by revising acute and obtuse angles and the use of a protractor. Encourage the children to test their predictions by gathering information about as many people as they can. In order to correctly measure their finger angles, the children should draw around their hand on a piece of scrap paper and then use a ruler to draw two straight lines as close to the finger edges as possible, ensuring that the lines meet at a point between the two fingers.

Developing Numeracy Using & Applying Maths Year 5 © A & C BLACK

Palindromic times

A **palindromic number** is one that is the same when you read it forwards and backwards. **Examples:** 414 737 1221

We can say that these digital clock times are **palindromic times**:

4:14   7:37   12:21

- **Predict how many palindromic times a digital clock shows between midnight and midday.**

- **Now test your prediction.**

Try to be systematic.

My prediction

_____ times

Some clocks show times with a zero in front of a single-digit hour. Example: 04:40 instead of 4:40

- **Investigate the number of palindromic times on a clock like this.**

Teachers' note For the main activity, the children should list times without including a zero in front of single-digit hours, i.e. 6:30 rather than 06:30. Ensure that they think carefully about whether a palindromic number is actually a real time, and encourage them to work systematically to investigate the number of palindromic times within each hour period. As a further extension, more confident children could explore palindromic times on a 24-hour clock.

**Developing Numeracy
Using & Applying Maths
Year 5
© A & C BLACK**

What's my card?

On each card, there are two lines and a dot.

• Try this activity with a partner.

☆ Cut out the cards. Spread them out face down.

☆ Pick a card. Describe the diagram for your partner to draw it on a piece of paper.

☆ Compare the drawing with your card. Is it accurate?

Use words like these.

parallel	perpendicular	right angle	horizontal	vertical	diagonal
curved	straight	end	halfway	mid-point	crossing	length

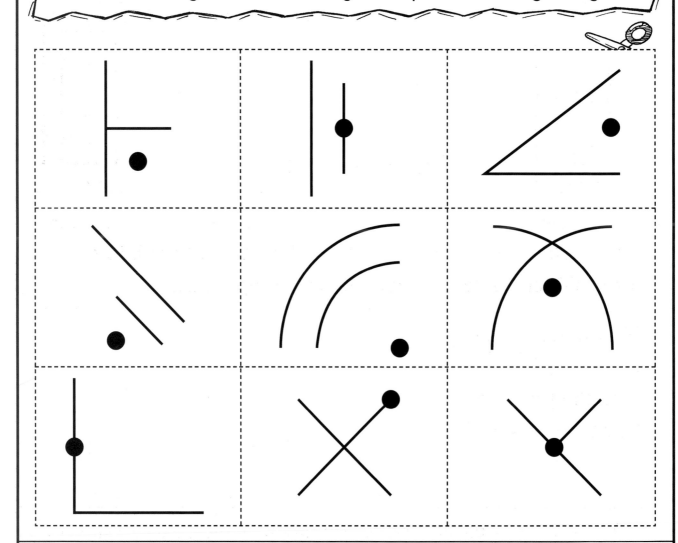

Now try this!

• Write a description of each card so that someone else could pick it from the set.

Teachers' note Provide one sheet per pair, ideally copied onto card so that the diagrams cannot be seen through the paper. As a further extension, ask the children to talk to each other about the cards and to decide how they would like to sort them into groups. Accept any ways of sorting, encouraging the children to explain their reasoning to others. The cards could be stuck onto separate pieces of paper in their sets and displayed for further discussion.

**Developing Numeracy
Using & Applying Maths
Year 5
© A & C BLACK**

One man went to mow...

Look for patterns and reason

This lawn is 5 m wide and 10 m long.
A man mows the lawn with a mower
that is exactly 1 m wide.
There are different ways
he could mow the lawn.
Here is one way. ⟶

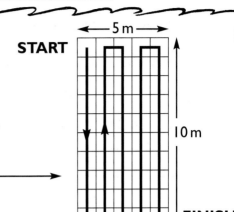

START

5 m

10 m

FINISH

- **Finish each route. Work out how far the man walks each time.**

A
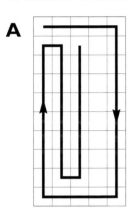
_____ m

B
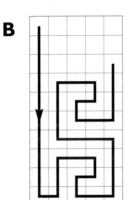
_____ m

C
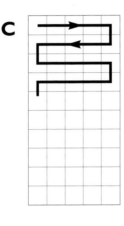
_____ m

D
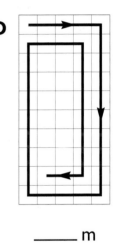
_____ m

- **Now look at the distance from the finish point back to the start. Which route requires least walking?** _____

- **Find a route that is exactly** 50 m **, including walking back to the start.**

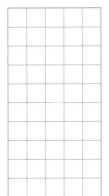
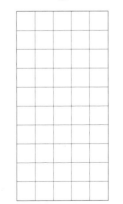
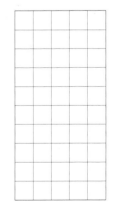

Now try this!

- **Draw a different-shaped lawn. Investigate which route requires least walking.**

You need squared paper.

Teachers' note When calculating the distance for each route, ensure that the children count from the middle of each square to the next. Encourage them to try to give reasons for the things they find out. Draw attention to the number of square metres on the lawn and the distance each route requires. When the routes include walking back to the start, the children should explore routes that finish as close as possible to the start (see page 12). Provide squared paper for the extension activity.

**Developing Numeracy
Using & Applying Maths
Year 5
© A & C BLACK**

The Dark Ages

Make decisions

You need a calculator.

- **Which of the people hidden in this castle are older than you? With a partner, discuss how you could find out. Then tick the correct boxes.**

I am 400 million seconds old.

I am 5 million minutes old.

I am 80 000 hours old.

I am 4000 days old.

I am 500 weeks old.

I am 100 months old.

- **Now write your own approximate age in:**

days	hours	minutes	seconds

Now try this!

- **Work out <u>exactly</u> how many days old you are. Remember, every year that is a multiple of 4 has 366 days.**

You need a calendar.

Teachers' note Encourage the children to explain the method they used to solve the problems. For the extension activity, remind the children that you are part-way through a year, so they should take into account the date of their birthday and add on the extra days. Also, leap years should be considered. The results can be listed in order on the board for comparison. Ask questions such as: 'Whose number of days will be a multiple of 10/25/50/100 next? How many days away is this?'

Developing Numeracy
Using & Applying Maths
Year 5
© A & C BLACK

A lengthy challenge

• **Work in a small group.**

• **Together, agree on** estimates

  for these lengths.

Remember to write a unit for each estimate.

the width of your teacher's thumb	the distance from the classroom to the staff room	the height of your teacher's chair
estimate _____	estimate _____	estimate _____
actual _____	actual _____	actual _____
the width of the board	the depth of the rubbish bin	the height of the board
estimate _____	estimate _____	estimate _____
actual _____	actual _____	actual _____
the distance around the outside of the rubbish bin	the height of the tallest child in your class	the distance from the board to the back of the room
estimate _____	estimate _____	estimate _____
actual _____	actual _____	actual _____
the width of the door	the thickness of the door	the width of the light switch
estimate _____	estimate _____	estimate _____
actual _____	actual _____	actual _____

Now try this!

• **Tick the three estimates you are most confident about.**

• **Now find all the actual measurements.**

• **Which of your estimates were closest?**

Teachers' note Once all the groups have written their estimates, work together as a class to measure and find the answers. The groups could swap papers to ensure that estimates do not get changed. Encourage the children to say what they think is an acceptable margin of error for each item and allocate points: for example, two points for an estimate that is exact and one point if it lies within a certain range of the measurement.

**Developing Numeracy
Using & Applying Maths
Year 5
© A & C BLACK**

Time to reflect

Visualise and generalise

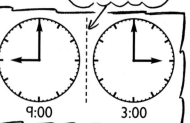

mirror line

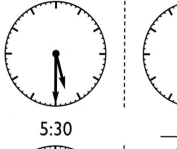 **You need** a clock and a mirror.

If you look at a clock in the mirror, it can look like another time of the day.

9:00   3:00

• **Draw and write the reflection of each time.**

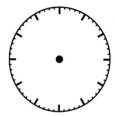   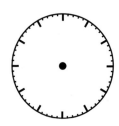      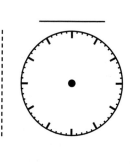

5:30   _____   11:15   _____

   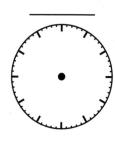      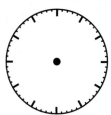

7:45   _____   4:10   _____

• **Find other pairs of times that are reflections of each other.**

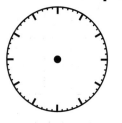   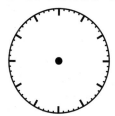   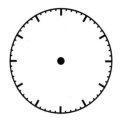   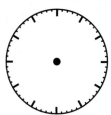

_____   _____   _____   _____

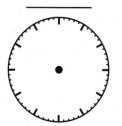   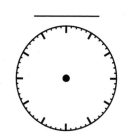   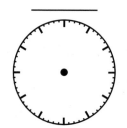   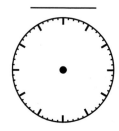

_____   _____   _____   _____

• **Write a rule for finding the reflection time of any time of day.**

 Now try this! • **Use your rule to write more pairs of times that are reflections of each other.**

Teachers' note The children will need real clocks and mirrors. Draw attention to the position of the hour hand for times between the 'o'clock' times (for example, the hour hand at 5:15 is a quarter of the way between 5 and 6). When the children try to write the rule, encourage them to list pairs of times and to examine the similarities and differences (see page 12 for rule). Discuss the different rules that the children come up with, and show that a rule can be written in more than one way.

**Developing Numeracy
Using & Applying Maths
Year 5
© A & C BLACK**

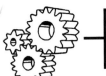

Trying tiles

Visualise and look for patterns

- **Work with a partner.**

  Each tile can be arranged in four ways:

  1 ◻ 2 ◻ 3 ◻ 4 ◻

- **Cut out the tiles at the bottom of the sheet.**

  Arrange them in a 4 × 4 grid to make the patterns below.

- **The numbers tell you which way up to put each tile. Fill in the numbers for each pattern.**

I	I	I	I
I	I	I	I
I	I	I	I
I	I	I	I

3	4		

- **Investigate some patterns of your own and the arrangements of the numbers.**

  You need squared paper.

Teachers' note This sheet provides a way to begin an investigation using 16 identical tiles. The children will need squared paper. Using numbers to record the orientation of the tiles can lead the children to explore, record and quickly compare patterns. The children can write their own sets of numbers and then see what the patterns will look like.

Developing Numeracy
Using & Applying Maths
Year 5
© A & C BLACK

43

Diagonal cuts

A **diagonal** is drawn on this 3 by 4 rectangle.

The diagonal cuts through six of the squares.

- Draw a diagonal on each rectangle.

- Shade the squares the diagonal cuts through.
  Write how many squares are shaded.

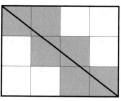

6 squares

2 by 3

_____ squares

4 by 2

_____ squares

3 by 5

_____ squares

4 by 4

_____ squares

You need a ruler and a sharp pencil.

- Draw some rectangles of your own. Look for patterns in the number of squares the diagonal cuts through.

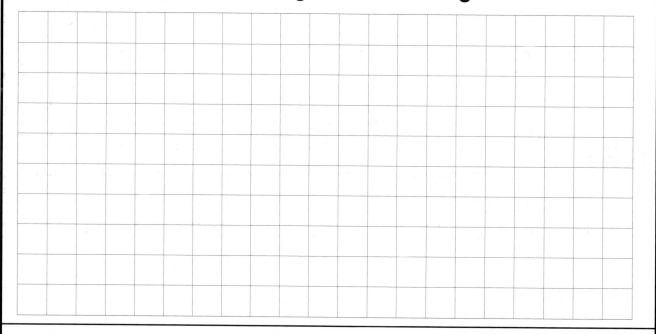

Now try this!

- **Talk to a partner about what you notice.**

- **How can you predict the number of squares a diagonal will cut through for different rectangles? Together, write some rules. Test your predictions.**

Teachers' note Ensure the children understand that they must shade and count all the squares that the diagonal passes through. Remind them that diagonals should be drawn accurately using a sharp pencil, otherwise the line may pass through more squares than it should. Provide additional squared paper so that the children can investigate larger rectangles.

**Developing Numeracy
Using & Applying Maths
Year 5
© A & C BLACK**

Friday the 13th

Test your ideas and generalise

- **Is there a Friday the 13th in the calendar year shown?** _____
- **In which month(s) do any occur?** _____

January						
Su	M	Tu	W	Th	F	Sa
						1
2	3	4	5	6	7	8
9	10	11	12	13	14	15
16	17	18	19	20	21	22
23	24	25	26	27	28	29
30	31					

February						
Su	M	Tu	W	Th	F	Sa
		1	2	3	4	5
6	7	8	9	10	11	12
13	14	15	16	17	18	19
20	21	22	23	24	25	26
27	28					

March						
Su	M	Tu	W	Th	F	Sa
		1	2	3	4	5
6	7	8	9	10	11	12
13	14	15	16	17	18	19
20	21	22	23	24	25	26
27	28	29	30	31		

April						
Su	M	Tu	W	Th	F	Sa
					1	2
3	4	5	6	7	8	9
10	11	12	13	14	15	16
17	18	19	20	21	22	23
24	25	26	27	28	29	30

May						
Su	M	Tu	W	Th	F	Sa
1	2	3	4	5	6	7
8	9	10	11	12	13	14
15	16	17	18	19	20	21
22	23	24	25	26	27	28
29	30	31				

June						
Su	M	Tu	W	Th	F	Sa
		1	2	3	4	
5	6	7	8	9	10	11
12	13	14	15	16	17	18
19	20	21	22	23	24	25
26	27	28	29	30		

July						
Su	M	Tu	W	Th	F	Sa
					1	2
3	4	5	6	7	8	9
10	11	12	13	14	15	16
17	18	19	20	21	22	23
24	25	26	27	28	29	30
31						

August						
Su	M	Tu	W	Th	F	Sa
	1	2	3	4	5	6
7	8	9	10	11	12	13
14	15	16	17	18	19	20
21	22	23	24	25	26	27
28	29	30	31			

September						
Su	M	Tu	W	Th	F	Sa
				1	2	3
4	5	6	7	8	9	10
11	12	13	14	15	16	17
18	19	20	21	22	23	24
25	26	27	28	29	30	

October						
Su	M	Tu	W	Th	F	Sa
						1
2	3	4	5	6	7	8
9	10	11	12	13	14	15
16	17	18	19	20	21	22
23	24	25	26	27	28	29
30	31					

November						
Su	M	Tu	W	Th	F	Sa
		1	2	3	4	5
6	7	8	9	10	11	12
13	14	15	16	17	18	19
20	21	22	23	24	25	26
27	28	29	30			

December						
Su	M	Tu	W	Th	F	Sa
				1	2	3
4	5	6	7	8	9	10
11	12	13	14	15	16	17
18	19	20	21	22	23	24
25	26	27	28	29	30	31

The year <u>before</u> the one shown was a | leap year | **.**

- **In the year <u>after</u> the one shown, what day of the week is:**

1st January? _____   12th January? _____

27th January? _____   9th February? _____

16th July? _____   15th December? _____

- **In which months will there be a Friday the 13th?** _____

Now try this!

- **Is there a Friday the 13th every year?**
How can you find out?

Teachers' note The calendar shown is for 2005. You may need to discuss leap years with your class to ensure that they understand the effect this can have on the days of the week particular dates fall on. As a further extension, the children could explore the days of the week their birthday will fall on over the coming ten years. Encourage them to investigate whether their birthday will fall on all the days of the week over a ten-year period.

Developing Numeracy
Using & Applying Maths
Year 5
© A & C BLACK

Overground map

Visualise and record information

The London Underground map shows the stations you can travel between, but it is <u>not</u> drawn to scale.

Dots show the main places. Lines show where you can get directly from one place to another.

Here is a similar map of a school.

It shows where you can walk.

• **Talk to a partner about this map.**

> Between which places can you walk directly?

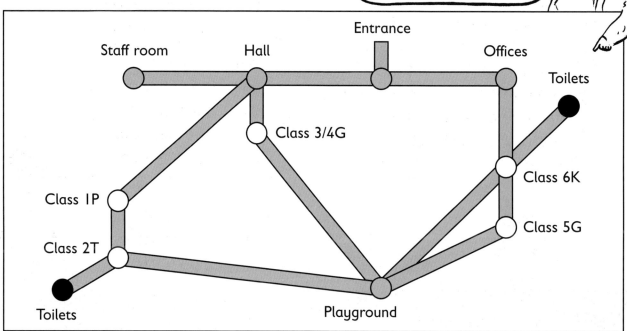

Staff room   Hall   Entrance   Offices   Toilets

Class 3/4G

Class 6K

Class 1P

Class 5G

Class 2T

Toilets   Playground

• **On a large sheet of paper, draw a similar map of your school.**

☆ Start by drawing circles to show places in the school.

☆ Then decide whether you can walk directly from one place to another (without going through another place). If you can, draw a straight line between the two circles.

☆ Are there any places in your school where teachers are allowed to walk, but children are not? You could use different-coloured lines to show this.

Now try this!

• **Compare your map with a partner's. Discuss the similarities and differences.**

Teachers' note If possible, show the children a map of the London Underground and ensure they appreciate that the idea is not to draw an exact plan, but to use straight lines to indicate whether a direct route is possible. For a large, many-roomed school, this activity could be simplified by asking the children to draw a map for, say, ten rooms in the school. Encourage use of coloured pencils (for example, the circles for cloakrooms/toilets could be one colour, the classrooms another, and so on).

**Developing Numeracy
Using & Applying Maths
Year 5
© A & C BLACK**

Shape shifters: 1

☆ Cut out the shapes below.

☆ Arrange them to make different patterns.

☆ Use *Shape shifters: 2* to record the patterns you make.

You can turn shapes over if you want to.

• **Investigate these questions.**

1. How many different patterns can you make?

2. Is it possible to make any shapes that have **reflective symmetry**?

3. Using six of the pieces, can you make a star? What do you notice when you rotate the star by 60°?

4. Join three pieces. What is the smallest number of sides the new shape can have?

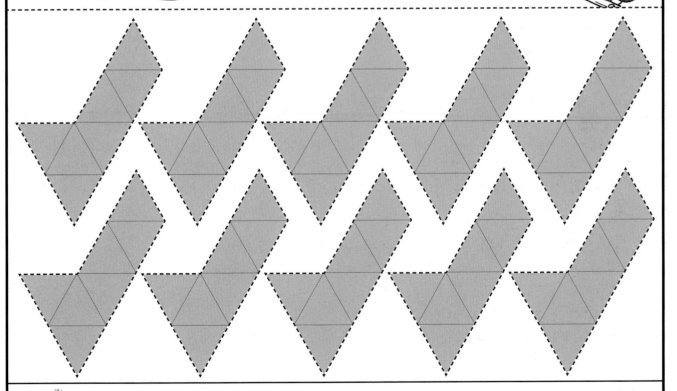

• **How many different ways can you use pieces to make a star shape?**

Teachers' note Copy this sheet onto thin card if possible. The children will need copies of page 48 to record the patterns they make. Ensure the children understand that the sides of the shapes should join and not overlap in any way. Demonstrate how the patterns that they make can be recorded on isometric paper. (See page 13 for examples of patterns that can be made.)

**Developing Numeracy
Using & Applying Maths
Year 5**
© A & C BLACK

Shape shifters: 2

Visualise, record information and use trial and improvement

• **Record your patterns here.**

One has been done for you.

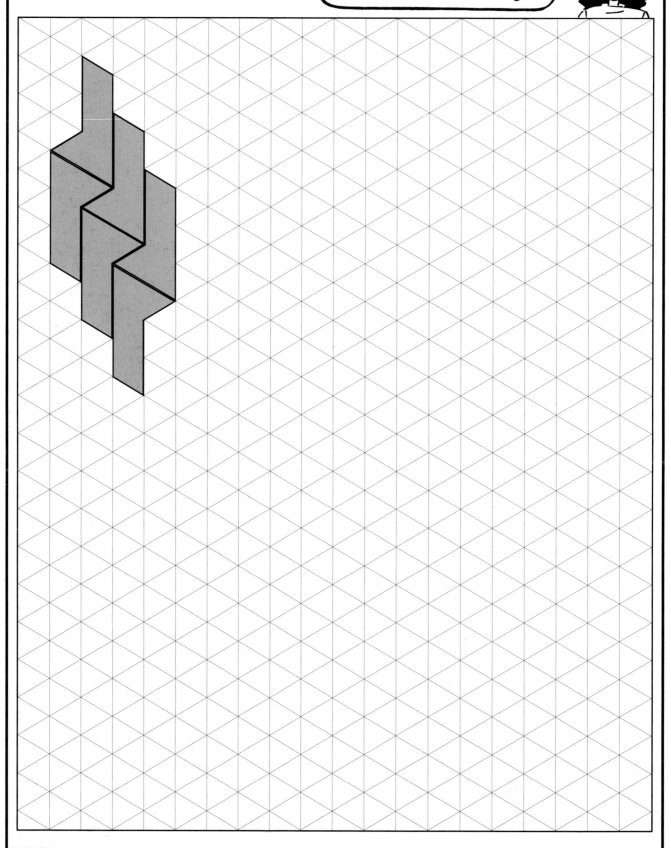

Teachers' note This sheet should be used in conjunction with page 47. Demonstrate how patterns can be recorded on this isometric paper, using the small triangles marked on the cut-out shapes to assist with this. Encourage the use of different-coloured pencils. Some children may benefit from this sheet being enlarged onto A3 paper. As well as investigating the questions on page 47, encourage the children to pursue their own lines of enquiry.

**Developing Numeracy
Using & Applying Maths
Year 5
© A & C BLACK**